Be the Best

TRACK & FIELD

A Step-By-Step Guide

By Gary Wright

Troll Associates

Library of Congress Cataloging-in-Publication Data

Wright, Gary.
    Track & field: a step-by-step guide / by Gary Wright.
        p.   cm.—(Be the best!)
    Summary: An introduction to the history and techniques of various
track and field events with advice on training and competition.
    ISBN 0-8167-1947-0 (lib. bdg.)   ISBN 0-8167-1948-9 (pbk.)
    1. Track-athletics—Juvenile literature.   I. Title.   II. Title:
Track and field.   III. Series.
GV1060.5.W75   1990
796.42—dc20   89-27344

Be the Best

TRACK & FIELD

A Step-By-Step Guide

FOREWORD

by Mel Rosen

To my mind, no sport in the world can compare with track and field. Why? Because any boy or girl can find a track-and-field event to enjoy doing. I've seen short athletes sprint and run distance, tall athletes hurdle and high jump, and heavy athletes throw the shot-put or discus. There's something for nearly everyone.

Track and Field, A Step-by-Step Guide, will teach you the basic skills and strategy you'll need to perform well. Then, with hard work, dedication, and perseverance, you can become a true champion—no matter who finishes first.

Good luck, and let's get started!

Mel Rosen

Mel Rosen is one of the most successful and respected track coaches in college history. He has been the head track coach at Auburn University since 1963. In that time, he has coached 125 All-Americans as well as 61 Southeastern Conference (SEC) outdoor and 56 indoor track champions. Under his coaching, Auburn's track team placed among the top ten finishers in both the NCAA indoor and outdoor championships every year between 1977 and 1981. In 1978, Mel was named NCAA and SEC Coach of the Year in both indoor and outdoor track. In 1984, he was the assistant coach for sprints, hurdles, and relays at the Olympic games in Los Angeles. There, the U.S. athletes he helped coach won 13 medals, including 7 gold.

Contents

Chapter	Title	Page
1	A Track Meet—The Ultimate Sports Competition	7
2	History of Track and Field	9
3	Equipment	13
4	A Track Stadium	15
5	Training for Track	18
6	Sprints or Dashes	25
7	Middle-Distance Running	33
8	Long-Distance Running	39
9	Hurdles	43
10	Relays	47
11	Field Events	50

A Track Meet—
The Ultimate
Sports Competition

A track meet is a busy beehive of sports action. A meet is made up of many small competitions called events. Several events are run or held at the same time. So something exciting is always happening on the field.

Track events include various sprints, distance runs, and leaping and jumping competitions. They also include strength competitions that require an athlete to throw a weighted object. Because of the varied events, a track team is made up of many different kinds of athletes. In track and field, there is something for everyone.

A track meet is both an individual and a team competition. Athletes compete individually in one or more events. Where they place in those events contributes points to the overall team effort. Only individuals can win events. But the team can win the meet if enough athletes place second or third in various competitions. An individual doesn't always have to finish first to help his or her team win. A track athlete can be a winner by always turning in his or her best effort. This book will teach you how to do your best in your chosen event.

History of
Track and Field

Many of the events in track and field are directly related to the survival skills of primitive humans. Long ago, prehistoric people jumped over bushes and streams while hunting for food. Hunters dashed after prey or ran long distances to escape predators. Rocks and spears were early weapons. They were hurled through the air like the modern shot-put and javelin.

As time passed, early humans sharpened their running, jumping, and throwing skills. The most athletic hunters won respect and honor. As life became more civilized and less dangerous, athletes no longer had to test their athletic skills against animals. So athletes began to compete against each other.

In ancient Greece, athletes were greatly admired. Cities often held competitions to determine their strongest and swiftest athletes. The winners became famous.

Sporting events became so popular in Greece that a special athletic contest was started in 776 B.C. The greatest athletes from all over Greece came to a place called Olympia to compete. The competition was called the Olympic games and was a huge success.

The nature of the Olympic games changed, however, after Rome conquered Greece in 146 B.C. They became less of a sport and more like organized combat. This continued until Roman Emperor Theodosius I finally ordered the Olympic games halted in A.D. 394.

Even though the Olympic games stopped for a time, track and field did not. Organized meets continued to be held down through the centuries. Track and field skills were too great a part of human nature to be ignored or forgotten.

In 1871, the first track meet in America was held in New York City. In 1876, the Intercollegiate Association of Amateur Athletes of America (ICAAAA) and the National Collegiate Athletic Association (NCAA) were formed. They are special athletic organizations that help govern track meets and other sporting events.

In 1896, the Olympic games were finally begun again after a 1,500-year absence. Baron Pierre de Coubertin of France helped organize the first modern Olympics. The games were held in April 1896 at Athens, Greece.

ANCIENT GREEK DISCUS THROWER

OLYMPIC SYMBOL

Since then, the modern Olympics have been held in a different country every four years. The best athletes from all over the world compete in the Olympic games. The motto of the modern Olympics is "Swifter, Higher, Stronger!" That is the goal of every track athlete.

Equipment

To run track, you do not need special equipment. Male and female runners usually wear shorts and tank tops or sleeveless T-shirts. For track meets, numbers are assigned to athletes and attached to the backs of their shirts.

SHOES

Some track runners wear special shoes. Track shoes should be very light. A track shoe has four to six sharp metal spikes on its sole. The spikes grip the track's surface to give the runner better traction.

SPIKED TRACK SHOES

However, track spikes can be dangerous! They are recommended for older, advanced runners only. Young runners can do just as well with ordinary sweat socks and sneakers.

A Track Stadium

A running track is oval shaped. It is made up of two long straight sections connected by two curved sections. Some tracks are 440 yards around (one-quarter mile). Today, most tracks measure four hundred meters.

A meter is the usual distance measurement in track. A meter is about three inches longer than a yard. A 400-meter track is about 437 yards 1 foot.

Painted on the surface of the track are lines separating it into lanes. There are also distance measurement marks that help in running certain events. (For example, the one hundred meters is a dash run down the straight end of the track, and its length is marked.)

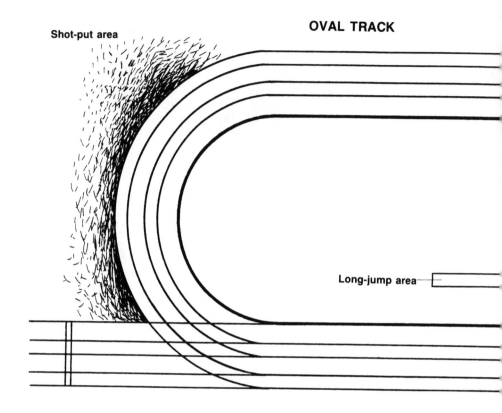

Shot-put area

Long-jump area

Some outdoor tracks are made of earth, clay, or cinders. Most modern tracks, especially indoor ones, are made of a special rubber and asphalt combined. They are known as all-purpose tracks. They need no special care and are not affected by bad weather. They are also just as soft as regular earth to run on, if not softer.

PLACE FOR FIELD EVENTS

Field events are usually held inside the track oval or just outside it. Some field events need special areas. The long-jump area has a long, narrow, all-weather

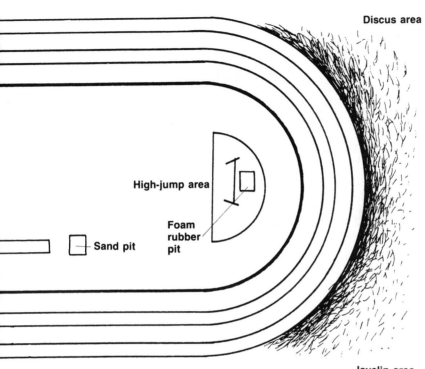

Discus area

High-jump area

Foam rubber pit

Sand pit

Javelin area

runway that leads to a large rectangular pit filled with sand.

The high-jump area is a large, clear area paved with rubberized asphalt. A huge foam rubber pit breaks the fall of the jumpers.

Special, circular areas of dirt or rubberized asphalt are used as launching areas for the shot-put and discus. The shot-put and discus are then tossed out onto grass or sod. The javelin is thrown on a large, open field.

Unofficial tracks can be marked out on flat, grassy playing surfaces. But the best place for a track meet is on a track.

Training for Track

A general track training program should include jogging, stretching, doing calisthenics, and conditioning.

JOGGING

Jogging is a slow, easy run used to warm up the body and to loosen up the muscles. It should always be the first part of any workout and should not be done in a sloppy, haphazard way. When you jog, concentrate on good running form.

As you jog, do not lean too far forward. Keep your head and chin up. Pump your arms rhythmically, keeping your elbows tucked into your sides. Your arms should move forward in a straight line and not across your chest. Keep your hands cupped.

JOGGING

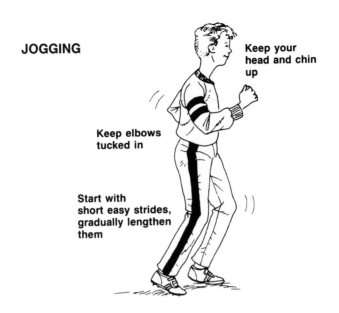

Keep your head and chin up

Keep elbows tucked in

Start with short easy strides, gradually lengthen them

Start with short strides. After you run a while, get your knees up and lengthen your stride. This way, you'll get full leg extension.

To start your workout, jog two times around the track. If you are not on a track, jog for a quarter or a half mile to begin.

STRETCHING

Stretching helps prevent muscle pulls, which can keep a runner out of action for weeks. Stretching is an important part of warming up and should be done slowly. Your coach or physical education teacher can show you several good stretching exercises. The stretches that follow are mainly for the legs.

Hamstring Stretch　The hamstring is a big muscle at the back of the leg. It runs from behind the knee to the bottom of the buttocks. It is frequently injured by runners who do not loosen up properly.

A simple way to stretch the hamstring is to stand with your feet spread. Cross one leg over the other so your feet are almost side by side. The outer parts of your feet should touch. Keeping the knees locked, bend at the waist. Touch your fingertips to your feet. Remain down for several seconds before slowly rising. Repeat at least three times. Then cross the other leg over the other foot, and repeat. If you do this hamstring stretch, you will feel the muscle loosening up behind your thigh. Any front bending done slowly with the knees locked will stretch the hamstring.

HAMSTRING STRETCH

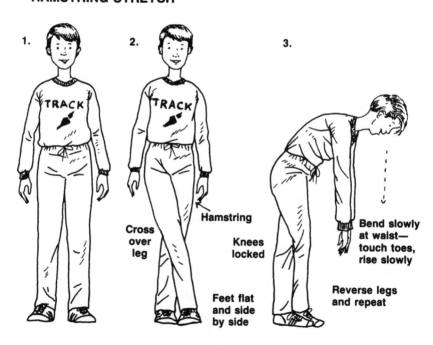

1.

2.

Cross over leg

Hamstring

Knees locked

Feet flat and side by side

3.

Bend slowly at waist— touch toes, rise slowly

Reverse legs and repeat

Starter Stretch   Crouch down with your hands on the ground. Extend one leg behind you, keeping the front of that foot on the ground and raising the heel. Keep your other foot flat on the ground. The knee of your front leg should be bent so it is close to your chest. Slowly lower the knee of your back leg to the ground. Switch legs and repeat three times.

STARTER STRETCH

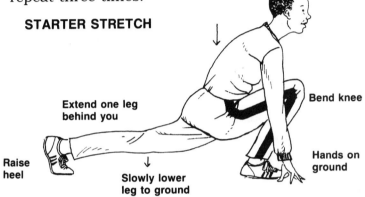

Hurdler's Stretch   This is another leg stretch. Sit on the ground with your legs extended. Bend one leg at the knee, folding it slightly under you and out to the side. Keep your other leg bent at the knee, toes pointed.

Slowly reach toward your pointed toes and bend your head toward your knee. Hold that position six seconds.

HURDLER'S STRETCH

1.

Touch hands to toes
and head to knee
2.

3.

Other hand
on ground

Sit on ground

Bend one
leg back to side

Grab other foot
and lean back

Return to a sitting position. Grab the foot of the bent leg with the hand on that side. Use the other arm and hand as a prop on the ground. Lean back slightly. Go only as far back as it is comfortable for you to do so. And do it slowly. After repeating three times, switch the positions of your legs and start over.

CALISTHENICS

Many people think runners only need to develop their leg muscles. That's not true. Arm and upper-body strength is also important to runners.

Exercises like chin-ups, pushups, and pull-ups are excellent strength builders. Fingertip pushups and deep pushups between chairs are also good ways to increase upper-body power.

For deep pushups, place two chairs near each other. Leave a space between them. Assume a pushup position with your hands on the chairs. Slowly dip your body into the gap between the chairs, then push up. Be careful not to go too low.

DEEP PUSHUP

Dip body slowly

Don't go too low

CONDITIONING

Being in good condition will help improve your strength, speed, endurance, and mental alertness. It will also reduce the chances of serious injury during competition.

Of course, jogging, stretching, and calisthenics all contribute to good conditioning. But there are two other ways you can build conditioning as you train for track: running corners and pickups.

Running Corners While taking laps around the track, alternate speeds. Down the straight-away, always run at half speed. Around the corners of the track, get up to your top speed. Stay at top speed until you reach the next straight-away. Slow down on the straight-away. Running laps this way builds endurance. The number of laps you do is up to your coach and you.

Pickups These are a special kind of lap. As you run the lap, you gradually increase your speed. It is best to do it down the straight-away. As you pick up your speed, raise your knees higher. Lean your body a bit more forward. Pump your arms in a relaxed way. They should go straight out, not across your chest. Your lead arm should reach no higher than your navel. Your opposite hand should not go farther back than your hip. Keep your body relaxed, and breathe through your mouth and nose. Walk the curve and repeat three times.

SPRINTER DOING PICKUPS

Lean forward

Pump
arms
easily

Raise knees
as you
pick up
speed

Gradually increase your speed. Do not go all out to start. When you reach top speed, continue at top speed for thirty meters. Then slow down gradually until you reach a nice, easy jog. Only after you become completely relaxed should you attempt to do another pickup.

Sprints or Dashes

Sprint distances are from 55 meters to 200 meters. A 55 meter sprint is usually an indoor race. Most outdoor high school meets use sprint distances of 100 meters and 200 meters.

A sprint is a short race. Sprinters have to run very fast. They come in all shapes and sizes. Short sprinters usually run best at distances from 55 meters to 100 meters. Taller sprinters with longer strides usually run best at distances from 100 to 200 meters.

SPRINTING FORM

In order to be a sprinter, you have to have natural speed. The secret of being a good sprinter is having a long stride that carries you low to the ground. Using correct form will also make you a better and faster runner.

Becoming a good sprinter starts by getting your knees up high when you run. Reach out with your front leg, stretching it out before it touches the ground. That helps increase your stride. Run high on your toes and push off them as you come up. Thrust forward, *not* up, as you move.

As you move, run tall. That means keeping your back straight and your hips forward. Try to maintain a slight forward lean.

The arm swing is also very important. Your arms should swing from the shoulders and go parallel to the track. Do not swing them across your chest. The arm pump should not reach any higher than your navel or go farther back than your hip. That will keep you low to the ground.

Finally, be relaxed and breathe easily. Keep your jaw and hands loose. Do not gulp breaths of air.

SPRINTING FORM

Run tall

Slight forward lean

Keep back straight
and hips forward

Swing arms from shoulders

Swing back arm
to hip, not further

Arm swings straight,
not higher than navel

Knees high

Reach out with front leg,
stretching it out before it
hits the ground

Long,
low stride

Run high on
your toes

STARTING BLOCKS

Sprinters and some other runners use special starting blocks. The blocks are adjustable and anchored to the track. Runners fit their feet against the blocks. Starting blocks give runners a solid base to push off from. They should always be placed so your feet are directly behind your hips.

STARTING BLOCKS

CROUCH START

In a short race like a sprint, a good start is often the difference between winning and losing. So practicing your starts is important.

The crouch start enables a sprinter to bunch his or her leg muscles for a powerful start that will shoot him or her quickly off the mark. It also launches the body forward in a half-horizontal position that cuts down air resistance during the first few strides.

To start, drop to a crouch position with your fingertips on the ground. Keep your hands spread a bit wider than shoulder width. If you are right-handed, your left knee is up and forward. Fold your left foot under you so your heel touches the back of your leg where the thigh joins the buttocks. Your right leg should be back farther, and

CROUCH START

A. RIGHT-HANDED RUNNER

B. LEFT-HANDED RUNNER

Left knee up

Right knee up

Rest knee on ground

Right heel touching back of right buttock

Thumbs in

your knee should rest on the ground. Keep your right heel under your seat. (Reverse this process if you're left-handed.)

Place your hands inches behind the starting line. Raise your palms, propping them up by the fingertips. The thumbs point toward each other, and your weight should be on the knee that is down.

This is the position a sprinter should assume when the starter shouts, "Get on your mark."

Once you are in this position, concentrate. Listen for the starter's commands. Do not look around.

SET CALL

The starter's next call will be "Set." The sprinter then raises his or her seat off the ground until it is shoulder level. The head remains down. Your weight should be distributed so that it rests equally on your hands, on your front leg, and on your back leg. As you rise, your heels should be off the ground and your rear leg should be slightly extended.

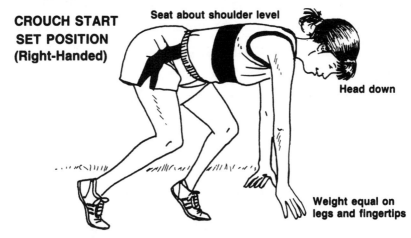

CROUCH START SET POSITION (Right-Handed)

Seat about shoulder level

Head down

Weight equal on legs and fingertips

SET POSITION FRONT VIEW

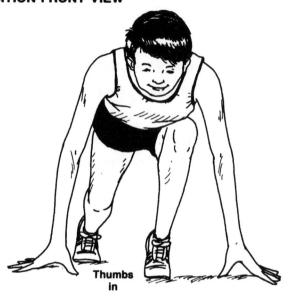

Thumbs in

GO!

Do not anticipate the starting gun or the "Go" call. If you start before the gun is fired, that is called a false start.

At the sound of the starting gun, move straight ahead out of the crouch. This first movement is forward, not upward. If you're right-handed, your left arm goes out and forward as your right arm swings back. Your right leg or back leg steps first. Here, your stride is short. Your left leg pushes off and takes a short step. (If left-handed, reverse this process.)

Stay slightly crouched for the first few steps. Swing your arms forward, not up. Get your knees high. As you run, lengthen your strides or "stretch out" down the straight-away.

START FROM CROUCH
(Right-Handed)

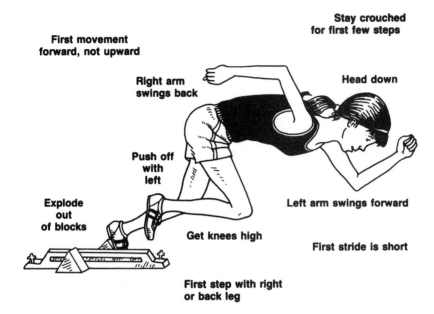

Stay crouched for first few steps

First movement forward, not upward

Right arm swings back

Head down

Push off with left

Explode out of blocks

Left arm swings forward

Get knees high

First stride is short

First step with right or back leg

RUNNING

As you sprint, your strides should get faster and longer. Remember to use good sprinting form (see page 25). You should reach full stride about fifteen or twenty meters down the course.

Remember, in a sprint you *must* stay in your own lane. Do not run out of your lane or you will be disqualified.

Also keep your sight set on the finish. Look straight ahead. Do not look around.

A sprinter should lean about twenty-five degrees forward through the race. Maintaining stride and form is important.

As you move down the last twenty meters you should be relaxed and confident. Do not slow up.

FINISHING

Always sprint *through* the finish line. Do not slow up or coast. The first runner to hit the tape with some part of his or her body from waist to upper chest wins. Many runners lean even more forward at the finish. A good habit is always to run five meters past the finish line.

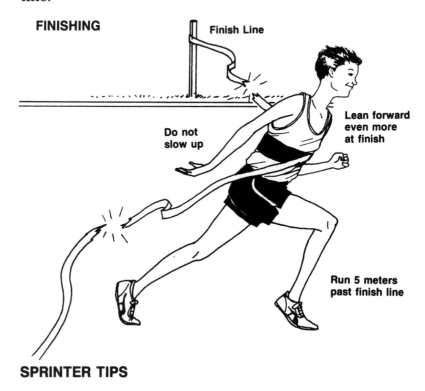

FINISHING

Finish Line

Lean forward even more at finish

Do not slow up

Run 5 meters past finish line

SPRINTER TIPS

A sprinter's work should include running distances of two hundred to three hundred meters at three-fourths speed and then sprinting full speed for fifty or sixty meters from a slow running start. (Also see page 28.) Running timed 400-meter laps (once around the track) is also good training.

Middle-Distance Running

The middle-distance races are the 400-meter dash and the 800-meter run. There are differences in how they are run. However, the qualities all middle-distance runners need are speed, stamina, good running form, and the self-discipline to pace oneself wisely.

400-METER DASH

The 400-meter dash is a one-lap race around an oval track. The 400-meter dash is a combination of a sprint and a distance race. It is a difficult race to run.

Because the race is a long one, pacing is important. Usually, 400-meter dash runners race at top speed for the first sixty to one hundred meters. After that, they slow slightly into what is called a "fast float." Floating is running with no excess strain on the arms or legs. A runner's stride is slightly longer than that for a short race. It is a swift but relaxed running style that takes practice to master. Runners usually float for about 200 meters or so.

FLOATING

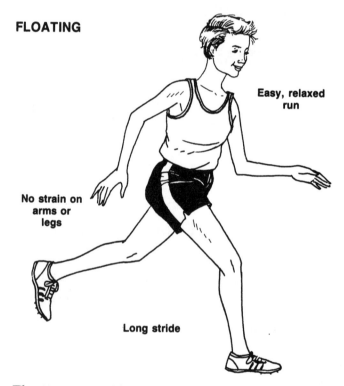

Easy, relaxed run

No strain on arms or legs

Long stride

Floating gives 400-meter dash runners a chance to save a bit of energy for the finish. In the last 100 meters of the 400-meter dash, the runners sprint for the tape. And they always run through the finish line (see page 32).

400-METER RUNNER

Carry head high

Lean slightly

Knees lower
than sprint

For the most part, 400-meter dash runners use a sprinting form (see page 25). However, the longer the race is, the lower the knee is lifted on each stride. The body lean is also less (about fifteen degrees forward) and the head is carried high.

400-METER DASH TIPS

In training for the 400-meter dash, runners should run 300- or 600-meter laps and sprint the last sixty to eighty meters. They should also work on their starts.

800-METER DASH

The 800-meter run, or half mile, is two laps around the oval track. It is an exciting race to watch—swift and full of strategy.

800-meter runners start from a standing position. In the standing start, the runner is behind the line with one foot slightly forward. (It is usually the left foot for right-handed runners, and vice versa for left-handed runners.) The back foot has the heel slightly raised. The runner leans a bit forward, but enough weight remains on the back foot to give a good push-off.

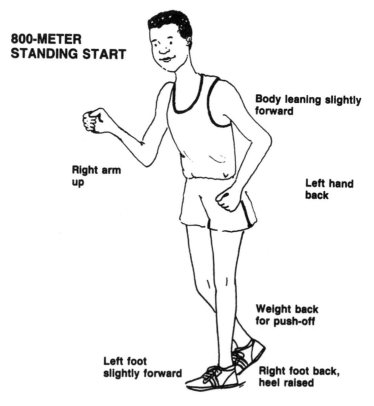

800-METER STANDING START

Body leaning slightly forward

Right arm up

Left hand back

Weight back for push-off

Left foot slightly forward

Right foot back, heel raised

Once the race starts, runners jockey for position. The runners are not required to remain in their lanes. Most try to run in the lane closest to the inside of the track because it is a shorter distance to run than the outside lanes.

During the 800-meter run, runners must pace themselves. Some like to lead, while others like to trail the leader. In trailing the leader, you should take a position at the outside right shoulder of the leader. That will prevent other runners from boxing you in.

During a race, you should try not to pass or be passed too many times. Passing takes up a lot of energy. Find a comfortable position in the pack and maintain it. Stay with the leaders and save enough strength to sprint at the finish.

The running form for the 800-meter run is like the 400-meter dash (see page 35). Again, the body lean is about fifteen degrees forward. The head is carried high. The knees do not go too high on each stride, and the arm swing is lower.

EUROPEAN STRIDE

Front leg strikes ground while knee is slightly bent

AMERICAN STRIDE

Lead leg strikes ground with knee straight

The position of the lead leg as it strikes the ground can vary. If the lead foot strikes the ground with the knee still slightly bent, that is called the "European stride." If the lead foot strikes the ground with the knee and leg straight from hip to toe, that is called the "American stride." Whichever stride works better for you is the one you should use.

800-METER RUN TIPS

A typical workout for an 800-meter runner might be jogging (see page 18), stretching (see pages 19-22), pickups (see page 23), pace work (200-meter sprints and 400-meter dashes), and still more jogging.

Long-Distance Running

Until recently, many people thought long-distance runners were athletes who were too slow for other races. But that is hardly the case. Many long-distance runners began as 400-meter or 800-meter runners. Once they mastered those middle distances and ran them with ease, they moved up to the mile or longer distances. Long-distance runners are special athletes. They must be well-conditioned and determined. And they must know how to run a smart race.

THE MILE OR 1500 METERS

A mile race is four laps around an oval track. Mile runners use a standing start (see page 36). The race usually starts briskly but settles down into a nice, easy pace after about twenty to thirty meters. At the start of a race, most milers jockey for positions where they can operate according to their own strengths.

Some like to lead and set the pace, and some like to be just behind the leader. Others prefer to run just slightly behind in the pack. Mile runners do not get their knees up very high. Also, their arm swing is lower and there is more bend at the elbow.

MILERS IN PACK JOCKEY FOR POSITION

Run close to inside of track

Long-distance runners must conserve and use their energy wisely. Body movements should not be wild or jerky. Running relaxed is very important.

Some long-distance runners use the "European stride," while others use the "American stride" (see page 37). The part of the foot that strikes the ground also differs from sprints and middle distances. In long distances, the runner's heel and sole strike the ground rather than the ball or front of the foot.

Other accepted miler practices are not to look back and not to run wide on the curves. Try to hug the inside lane as much as possible.

MILE RUNNER

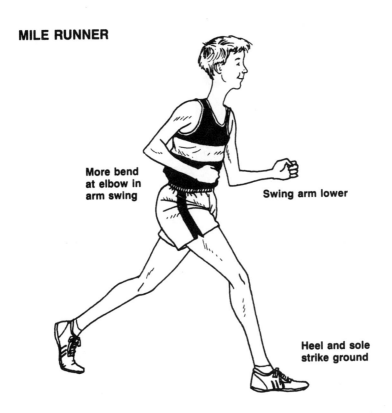

More bend at elbow in arm swing

Swing arm lower

Heel and sole strike ground

Another crucial part of long-distance running is breathing. Getting enough air will help you avoid muscle cramps and fatigue. Different coaches teach different breathing techniques. In general, it is best to breathe easily rather than inhaling and exhaling rapidly. If you inhale through both your mouth and your nose, you should get adequate oxygen.

KICK FINISH

In long distances, a runner's "kick" is important. This means having a reserve of energy so the runner can go strong and flat-out at the finish.

A MILER'S KICK

To run smart, milers pace themselves and save energy for a strong finish kick

Generally, a miler's last lap should be the fastest. Knowing where to start one's kick is a matter of trial and error. Each kick will differ for each individual. Only by running races can a miler learn where to start his or her kick.

LONG-DISTANCE RUNNING TIPS

A good way to prepare yourself for the mile is to run quick, shorter distances. Running a fast hundred yards and then jogging back and repeating that several times will get you in good condition for running the mile. You should also run three to four miles every other day.

9

Hurdles

There are two kinds of hurdle races. The high hurdles race is a short one, usually 110 meters. High hurdles are three feet six inches high. The intermediate hurdles race is 400 meters long. Intermediate hurdles measure three feet high. Each race has ten hurdles.

In high school, an intermediate race is usually 300 meters long. It also has eight hurdles instead of ten. High-school high hurdles are different too. They measure three feet three inches high for boys and two feet nine inches high for girls.

WHO HURDLES?

A high hurdler has the quickness of a sprinter, the leaping ability of a high jumper, and the stamina of a 400-meter dash runner. Most high hurdlers also run the intermediate hurdles.

Hurdlers come in all shapes and sizes. Most, though, are tall and slim.

HIGH HURDLES

In high hurdles racing, fourteen meters separate the starting line from the first hurdle. There are about nine meters between each of the remaining nine hurdles. And from the last hurdle to the finish line is a distance of fourteen meters. This total of 110 meters makes up the high hurdles race.

Running the high hurdles involves a series of running leaps over the hurdles. Running the low hurdles requires more of a lunge over the hurdles. It is much easier to adapt a high hurdler's form to a low hurdler's form than vice versa. So the high hurdling technique will be discussed in full below.

HURDLING

Out of the starting blocks, hurdlers use a sprinter's start (see pages 28-30). How many steps a runner takes to each hurdle is important. Older runners usually take about seven or eight strides to the first hurdle and about three strides between the other hurdles. For younger runners, the number of steps will depend on the length of your stride.

Run easily at the beginning, with your front leg slightly bent. Drive over the hurdle with your body leaning forward. The arm opposite the lead leg is the one that will cross the hurdle first. Keep your other arm at your side. Lead with whichever leg is more comfortable.

HIGH HURDLING

1. Lean forward — Knee almost straight — Lead leg extended, toes up

2. Trail leg bends to outside

3. Rear leg crosses in level position to hurdle

As you reach the hurdle, the lead leg extends forward with the knee almost straight. The toe is up and the heel is down. After your leap, the rear or trail leg bends to the outside as it leaves the ground.

The rear leg will cross the hurdle in a level position parallel to the top of the hurdle. The knee of the rear leg is bent so the heel of the foot almost touches the back of the thigh.

HIGH HURDLING LANDING

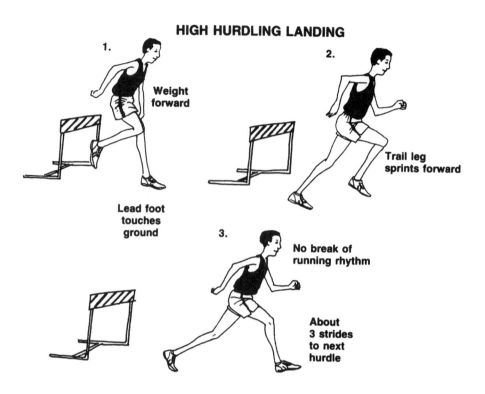

1. Weight forward

Lead foot touches ground

2. Trail leg sprints forward

3. No break of running rhythm

About 3 strides to next hurdle

Do not attempt to step over the hurdle or sail over it. You will lose valuable time. It is a running leap.

Your body lean position is important to leaping a hurdle. When you hit the ground on the other side of the hurdle, your body weight must be over or a bit in front of the lead leg. However, remember to keep your balance. When you land, be sure the lead foot touches first. Your back leg will then kick up to start the sprint into the next hurdle.

Beginning runners should make sure the same lead foot always goes over the hurdle first. That is why the steps a runner takes between each hurdle are important. After the first hurdle, the steps between each following hurdle should be the same.

Relays

There are several relay events at track and field meets. A relay is a team race where four different individuals each run a portion of the race. The first person to run is called the leadoff. The last person to run is called the anchor. The anchor is usually the fastest of the four runners.

Runners in a relay race must have basic running skills. They must also be able to pass the baton smoothly. A runner in a relay race cannot run until a teammate has passed him or her the baton. Effectively passing the baton can help win or lose the race.

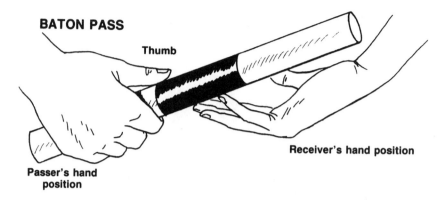

BATON PASS

Thumb

Receiver's hand position

Passer's hand position

The baton must be carried in the hand. And it must be passed to the next runner within a twenty-meter zone. A dropped baton must be recovered before a runner can proceed.

There are two types of baton passes: the visual pass and the blind pass.

VISUAL PASS

As the runner approaches, the receiver moves forward slowly, looking back over his or her right shoulder. The receiving arm is extended back toward the runner.

VISUAL PASS

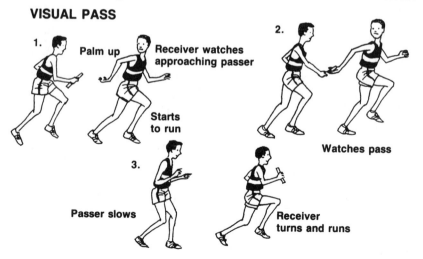

1. Palm up

Receiver watches approaching passer

Starts to run

2. Watches pass

3. Passer slows

Receiver turns and runs

The palm is up and the fingers are slightly spread. The runner reaches out and slaps the baton into the receiver's hand. The receiver watches to make sure the pass takes place. As the receiver moves ahead and gains speed, the passer allows the baton to slip free.

BLIND PASS

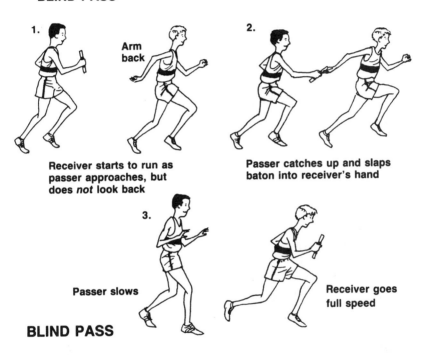

1. Arm back

Receiver starts to run as passer approaches, but does *not* look back

2. Passer catches up and slaps baton into receiver's hand

3. Passer slows

Receiver goes full speed

BLIND PASS

In the blind pass, the receiver watches the passer approach. He or she then turns away and begins to move forward when the runner is seven meters away. The receiver moves with the receiving arm extended back toward the passer. It is the passer's job to place the baton in the receiver's hand. The receiver does not watch the pass but continues looking forward. Once the pass is made, the receiver then pulls the baton out and takes off as the passer slows.

Field Events

Field events are just as popular as track events. The long jump, the high jump, the javelin throw, the discus throw, and the shot-put are exciting events to watch. And they're challenging events to perform. Most of these field events require the help of a qualified coach.

LONG JUMP

The long jump requires speed, agility, and springy legs. Long jumpers do not fit any one physical type. They can be tall, short, lean, or stocky.

There are four distinct parts to long jumping. The first part is the approach. Next is the takeoff. The airborne position follows. And then there is the landing. Each will be discussed separately.

The Pit The layout for a long jump consists of a long runway of forty or fifty meters leading to a special takeoff, or toe, board. The board is about two feet wide for high-school athletes but smaller for older athletes. Beyond the board is a soft landing pit about twenty-five feet in length. Usually it is filled with sand. This makes it easier for officials to measure the long jump, and it also helps cushion the landing of the long jumpers.

Takeoff Board You're allowed three jumps. All jumps are measured from the edge of the takeoff board nearest the pit, not from where the jumper actually takes off from. So the closer a jumper can take off to the end of the board, the longer the jump is likely to be. Stepping over the board's edge, however, is a foul. It cancels out the jump.

Approach Long jumpers should measure their approach to the takeoff board so they will hit the perfect takeoff mark and not foul or jump too early. The way to do that is to pace off the steps from your starting spot to the takeoff board before you jump.

A good way to start is to measure twelve paces back from the takeoff board and make a mark. Measure twelve more paces back from there and make another mark. Starting with both feet together at the second mark, you should hit full speed by the time your jumping foot is even with the first mark.

Always start your approach with the foot opposite your takeoff leg. Long jumpers take off on one foot, usually the one they feel is stronger.

THE LONG JUMP TAKEOFF

The running stride for the long jump is a sprinter's stride (see page 31). The knees are high and the arms pump vigorously. The last two steps to the board should be slightly shorter than the other strides. Remember, your approach speed is crucial.

Takeoff When your takeoff foot hits the toe board, your body should be almost erect. The final short strides you take in the approach will help you accomplish that. Your takeoff should be upward and forward, *not* just forward. It must also be smooth. After your takeoff leg comes outward, the opposite leg should extend forward as your arms and head swing upward.

In the Air At the peak of your jump, your back should be arched with your arms flung upward. Carry your legs in almost a sitting position but don't let them get too far in front. Your arms should *not* trail behind your body.

Landing When you land in the pit, your feet should be spread just slightly. Your back should be straight, with your head and arms forward.

Long jumps are measured from the edge of the take-off board to where your heels break the surface of the sand. However, if you fall or touch backward, your jump will be measured only up to that point, *not* to your heels. So be sure to fall forward, not backward. And make sure your arms and hands don't accidentally touch behind your body.

THE LONG JUMP LANDING

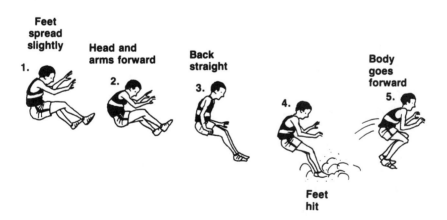

Long-Jump Tips Getting down a correct approach is crucial. So you should devote as much time as you can to practicing your approach and takeoff until both are second nature to you.

HIGH JUMP

The goal of a high jumper is to get his or her body up and over a raised bar without toppling it. High jumpers need good body control as well as leaping ability. A description of the high jump area is on page 17.

Techniques High jumping is an event that has many popular and accepted techniques. A key one is that a high jumper must take off from one foot. It is illegal to jump off of both feet. As in the long jump, you're allowed three jumps.

Marking a Takeoff Spot To mark a takeoff spot, stand facing the bar. Stretch out your arm so your fingertips can touch the bar. The point where you are standing is where you should take off from.

Scissors Kick The scissors kick is a very old technique that can be taught to beginners and then quickly discarded in favor of a more advanced jumping method.

In the scissors kick, a right-handed athlete approaches the bar from the right at an angle of ten to fifteen degrees. The jumper uses a seven- or eight-step approach. The jump starts with the right leg thrusting up as the left leg provides the spring and push-off. The right leg crosses the bar first, then the left leg. The jumper scissors his legs over the bar in a sitting position.

Fosbury Flop The "Fosbury flop" was created by Dick Fosbury, a 1968 U.S. Olympic champion in the high jump. It is one of the most popular high-jump techniques.

To do a "Fosbury flop," run toward the high-jump bar, curving to run alongside the bar for the last few steps. If you want to jump off with your left leg, start by running toward the right end of the bar and make your curve to the left. If you jump off with your right leg, start off at the left and curve to the right. In order to make the turn properly, lean away from the bar. Your last step should be a long one.

Place your foot about two to three feet from the bar and parallel to it, then spring upward. As you jump, twist so your back turns toward the bar. Go over the bar backward, headfirst.

Arch your back, and tilt your head backward as it goes over. This will help your shoulders, back, and hips to clear the bar. Once your hips are over the bar, tuck your chin into your chest. Doing this helps get your knees up and over the bar and also protects your head when you land. Be sure to land on your back, *not* your head or neck.

Do the "Fosbury flop" *only* if you have a foam rubber pit to land in and a qualified coach standing by.

Straddle Roll   The straddle roll is another popular high-jump roll. The approach is from a forty-degree angle. The push-off foot is planted almost at a right angle to the bar. The kick up is almost parallel to the bar, with the leg slightly bent. Drive your head and shoulders above the bar. Your body should cross the bar in a belly-down position rather than from a side position. Rotate your head and hips as you go over. Keep your front arm tucked elbow high.

Once your lead leg clears the bar, kick up your trail leg, bending it at the knee. This will cause you to roll over the bar. Keep your trail arm tucked tightly into your chest and land on your back.

STRADDLE ROLL

1. Kick up leg slightly bent

2. Drive head and shoulders above bar

3. Lead leg clears, trail leg bends

4. Face down, belly parallel to bar

5. Rotate head and hips, trail leg kicks up

6. Jumper rolls over bar, trail arm tucked tightly to chest

High-Jump Tips High jumping should *not* be practiced on your own. The techniques for high jumping are complicated and difficult to perform without proper supervision. High jumping should be taught by a trained coach and practiced under his or her watchful supervision.

JAVELIN THROW

The javelin is a long, hollow, spearlike shaft. It is not as easy to throw as it looks.

Grip The javelin has a whipcord binding in the center. To grip a javelin correctly, hold your palm upward, keeping your thumb toward your body. Hold the javelin at the binding firmly but not too tightly. Lay your thumb along the shaft, and rest your index finger on the cord binding. Your chief throwing fingers are the thumb and index finger. Carry the javelin at shoulder level with your elbow bent.

JAVELIN GRIP

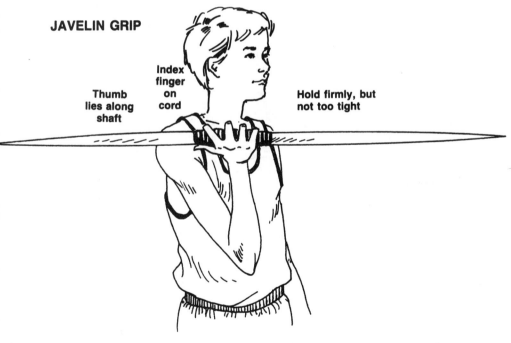

Thumb lies along shaft

Index finger on cord

Hold firmly, but not too tight

Throwing the Javelin Javelin throws are measured from a scratch line. The thrower cannot pass that point. Otherwise, it is a foul. You're allowed three throws.

Throwers run up to the scratch line and then throw. Most javelin throwers start with a running approach forty or fifty feet from the mark. The javelin is carried at the shoulder and then lowered into a special throwing position.

THROWING THE JAVELIN

1. Good balance

2. Drop arm, lowering javelin to waist high.

3. Arm slightly bent. Point up and away from body.

4. Torso twists. Right leg planted. Left leg crosses over and extends.

5. Left foot comes down. Body leans back to throw.

6. Right foot pushes off. Body and arm go forward.

7. Whiplike arm movement, snap wrist in follow-through.

All one fluid motion. Don't stop.

The running approach is like a sprinter's stride. Maintain good balance. About halfway to the scratch mark, you should be carrying the javelin at waist level. Make sure, however, that the front point is up and away from your body. Your arm should be slightly bent at the elbow but straight for the most part. As you near the scratch line, turn your body in position to make the throw.

Your torso should twist to the right. Plant your right leg as your body leans back. Keep the javelin tip held high. Your left leg then crosses over and extends into the air. As your left foot comes down, push off on your right foot and move your arm and body forward. This is the start of your throw. It must be one easy fluid motion, not a run and dead stop.

The throw itself is a whiplike arm movement. You should be holding the javelin at a forty-five-degree angle before your elbow leads the arm past your head. Then sling the javelin into the air with a final snap of your wrist. Your throw will be measured from the scratch line to where the tip breaks earth.

Caution! Throwing the javelin can be dangerous. Spectators have been seriously injured in some cases. Throw only under strict adult supervision and when and where you're supposed to.

DISCUS THROW

The discus is a weighted, saucerlike object thrown from a circle measuring eight feet two and a half inches in diameter. The high-school discus weight is three pounds nine ounces, two pounds eight ounces for girls. Hurling the discus is one of the oldest field events.

Holding the Discus The discus is held in a special way. Put the palm of your throwing hand flat across the surface of the discus. Spread your fingers. The first joint of your fingers should curl under the lip of the discus and hook around the edge. Then bend your hand at the wrist. This proper grip will allow the discus to skim through the air without much of a wobble.

Throwing the Discus There is also a special way to throw the discus. It is a spinning movement that takes lots of practice to master.

Stand in the throwing circle. You must stay in that circle while you throw. Otherwise, it is not a legal throw. You will throw three times only.

Start at the rear of the circle with your feet spread about shoulder width. Stand with your back facing the area you will throw into. Twist your upper torso at the waist by swinging your arms across your body, holding your hands low.

After several warm-up swings, plant your left leg and step over with your right leg toward the throwing area. (This is for a right-handed thrower.) Slightly bend your knees and hips. Extend your left arm for balance.

Your body should make one complete spin as you pivot onto the right foot. The right foot ends up planted with the toes still pointing away from the throwing area. The arm with the discus should be behind the back. You should again be facing away from the throwing field after the spin.

The next move is around and forward. Step toward the throwing area with your left foot. The left foot is planted flat with the toes aimed at the throwing area. The back (right) foot should now be used to push off. Bring your

DISCUS THROW

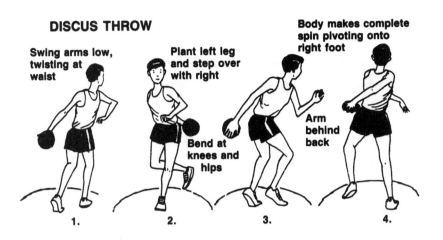

1. Swing arms low, twisting at waist

2. Plant left leg and step over with right — Bend at knees and hips

3. Body makes complete spin pivoting onto right foot — Arm behind back

4.

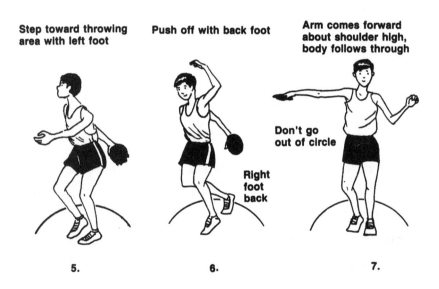

5. Step toward throwing area with left foot

6. Push off with back foot — Right foot back

7. Arm comes forward about shoulder high, body follows through — Don't go out of circle

arm forward with the discus. The discus should be extended out to the side at shoulder level and should come out of the hand off the index finger in a clockwise direction. The whiplike motion of your arm will send the discus sailing through the air. The follow-through will get your body into the throw. Your back (right) foot now comes forward but still *remains* in the throwing circle.

SHOT-PUT

The shot is the heavy metal ball used in the shot-put. It's heaved from a circle measuring seven feet in diameter.

Holding the Shot   The shot should be held in the palm of the hand with the fingers spread. Bend your arm at the elbow and rest the shot against your neck below the ear.

**HOLDING
THE SHOT**

Rests against neck
and below ear

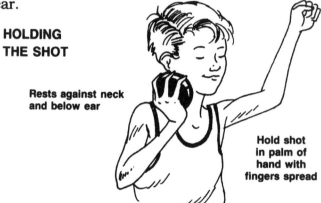

Hold shot
in palm of
hand with
fingers spread

Putting the Shot   The important thing to remember about the shot-put is that it is *not* a throw. You put, or heave, the shot. It is like pushing the shot away and into the air.

Holding the shot, stand in the shot-put circle at a right angle to the landing area. Spread your feet a bit wider than shoulder width. Tuck your throwing elbow in close to your side. Keep your other arm up for balance. Bend your right knee and dip your body into a crouch. Raise your left foot off the ground. As you push off your right foot, start to straighten your body and step toward the landing area with your left foot. Shift your weight forward.

PUTTING THE SHOT

Bend right knee and crouch — 1.

Raise left foot off ground — 2.

Push off with right foot — 3.

Straighten body and step toward landing area — 4.

5. **Shift weight forward. Turn head away from shot.**

6. **Push up. Extend arm.**

7. **Fingers snap, arm is fully extended**

Be sure to turn your head *away* from the shot or you will hit yourself with the throw. Do not take the shot away from your neck. Push your arm up at about a forty-degree angle. Your arm extension should be timed with the shift of your body weight forward. Do not let the shot leave your hand until your arm is fully extended. At the last moment, use your fingers to help snap it away. Remember not to fall out of the circle or it will cancel out your heave. You will heave the shot three times, with the longest legal one counting.

INDEX

Calisthenics / 22

Conditioning
    pickups / 22-23, 38
    running corners / 22

Discus / 11, 17, 59-61

Eight-hundred meter dash /
    35-38, 39

Equipment / 13-14

False start / 30

Field events / 16-17, 50-63

Fifteen-hundred meter run / 39-42

Finishing / 32

Floating / 34

Four-hundred meter dash /
    33-35, 39

High jump
    area / 17
    Fosbury flop / 54-55
    marking a takeoff spot / 54
    scissors kick / 54
    straddle roll / 55-56
    techniques / 54

History of track and field / 9-12

Hurdles / 43-46

Javelin / 9, 17, 57-59

Jogging / 18-19, 23, 24, 38

Kick finish / 41-42

Lanes / 15, 31, 36, 40

Long-distance running / 39-42

Long jump
    approach / 50, 51-52
    area / 16-17
    foul / 51

in the air / 50, 52-53
landing / 50, 53
pit / 17, 51
runway / 51
takeoff / 50, 52
takeoff board / 51, 52

Meets / 7, 10, 17, 25, 47

Middle-distance running / 33-38,
    39, 44

Mile race / 39-42

Olympic Games / 10-12

Relay races
    baton passing / 47-49
    blind pass / 49
    visual pass / 48-49

Set
    call / 29
    position / 29-30

Shot-put / 9, 17, 62-63

Spikes / 13-14

Sprints (dashes)
    finishing / 32
    form / 25-27, 31, 35
    starting / 28-30

Standing start / 36, 39

Starting
    blocks / 27, 44
    crouch / 28-31, 34

Stretch
    hamstring / 20
    hurdler's / 21-22
    starter / 21

Track stadium / 15-17